The Art of
Parchment Craft

To 'my girls' and Doug – thank you for your continued support and warm friendship, and for the pioneering spirit you have all shown in trying out the various techniques that I have come up with, helping me develop them into practicality by adding your own knowledge and experience.

I would like to thank John Dalton and Roz Dace, my editors, for all their help and support, and Dahler Rowney, for supplying the acrylic inks and paints.

The Art of
Parchment Craft

Janet Wilson

SEARCH PRESS

First published in Great Britain 1997

Search Press Limited
Wellwood, North Farm Road,
Tunbridge Wells, Kent TN2 3DR

Copyright © Janet Wilson 1997

Photographs by Search Press Studios
Photographs and design copyright © Search Press Ltd.
1997

5

Publishers' note
There is a reference to sable hair brushes in this book. It
is the publishers' custom to recommend synthetic
materials as substitutes for animal products wherever
possible. There are now a large number of brushes
available made from artificial fibres and they are just as
satisfactory as those made from natural fibres.

ISBN 0 85532 823 1

Tool sizes: all tools mentioned in this book are
manufactured to metric measurements. The
following is a list of the tools used together with
the nearest imperial equivalent.
1mm (0.040in)
1.5mm (0.060in)
3mm (0.120in)
4mm (0.160in)

If you have any difficulty in obtaining any of the
equipment or materials mentioned in this book,
then please write for further information to the
publishers.
Search Press Limited
Wellwood, North Farm Road,
Tunbridge Wells, Kent TN2 3DR

Printed in Spain by Elkar S Coop, Bilbao 48012

Contents

Bookmarks make small, useful presents for family and friends. This design echoes the medieval card design on pages 50–1, where you will find its pattern. Bookmarks are made using the same techniques and colours as for cards. Good print shops will laminate a bookmark for you, and you should be able to get two into one small laminate sleeve.

Introduction

The beautiful and ancient art of parchment craft is fast gathering a world-wide band of enthusiasts. The origins of this craft are somewhat obscure but it is believed to have developed from bookbinding as practised in Spain before Christopher Columbus discovered the 'new world'. Examples of early bookbinding from Spain, as well as France, can be seen in the British Library. Here, the parchment has been dipped into a medium that has made it translucent, and embossing and piercing has been skilfully applied to decorate the parchment – this is reminiscent of the basic principles of today's parchment craft.

The craft appears to have been taken to the Americas by the Church of Spain, following in the footsteps of the conquistadors. Since then, it has evolved from book-binding with parchment, to card- and box-making with translucent paper. Although the basic principles of embossing and piercing remain the same throughout the world, the style varies – Mexico, Brazil, Peru and Colombia, for example, all have distinct types of work.

The basic principles of parchment craft are embossing, perforating and cutting. No colour was used in the original craft with the exception of perhaps a little gold added to the design. Colouring the work is a twentieth-century addition and today's parchment crafters are divided into those who prefer the original white work and those who like the addition of colour.

One of the aims of this book is to show you the different methods you can use to add colour to your work. A chapter illustrating the embossing techniques of white work is followed by chapters showing how to use various forms of colour. Each contains step-by-step instructions; a practice sheet of patterns and a border which can be applied to any of the designs illustrated; and simple projects showing how to make gift cards, bookmarks, picture frames and even three-dimensional objects.

Materials

Parchment craft materials can be found in art and craft shops or via mail order specialists. Specially made paper-embossing and needle tools are used to create the beautiful patterns and lace-like designs shown throughout this book.

Parchment paper

This is a type of transcript paper (3). The weight most widely used is 140/150g. The paper should be fairly supple; some papers are brittle and they crack very easily when embossed, so try out a small piece first before investing in a large quantity.

Tracing

Pens (5)   You will need a mapping pen for non-metallic inks and I would recommend that you use a steel-nibbed pen for the metallic inks.

White pencil (6)   Use a white pencil to trace fine lines that require embossing. Embossing over white ink will make the traced line go black.

Embossing

Pads (4)   You can buy special embossing pads in different sizes. However, you can also use something like a padded diary – the sort with a plastic covering over a thin sponge insert.

Tools (7)   The working ends of these tools are small ball-shaped points of different sizes. In general, the smaller points produce the most intense white images (see page 11 for details of sizes used in this book). Similar tools are used for paper embossing.

Perforating

Pads (13)   Again you can buy perforating pads designed for this craft but you can use a piece of thick felt or a thick mouse mat, sponge side up. For multiple needle tools such as the 7-needle and half-circle tool, a thin rubber mat on a piece of cardboard works well.

Needle tools (12)   There are lots of different needle tools available. The patterns in this book are designed for tools with needles set 1mm apart. In certain parts of the world you can buy tools with thicker needles that are set slightly wider apart. If you use these larger tools, especially the 4-needle tool for lace borders, amend the designs to allow for the wider pitch. All the tools used in this book are illustrated on page 11.

Scissors (9)   Use curved cuticle scissors with very fine tips for cutting lace grids to crosses and slots. A pair of deckle-edged or pinking scissors can be used to trim the edges of some cards.

Colouring

Inks (1)   Use any waterproof or acrylic inks.

Paints (2)   Most types of acrylic paints work well.

Oil pastels (15)   There are a number of brands available on the market. You need to use ones that do not 'crumb'. Use odourless barbecue igniter or white spirit as a spreading medium.

Watercolour pencils (11)   There are a number of brands on the market and most work well.

Felt-tip pens (10)   Any water-soluble felt-tip pens can be used to good effect.

Brushes (8)   You will need a No. 2 acrylic or sable brush. You will also find a spotter and a No. 4 shader brush useful.

Other materials

You will also need a ruler (14), some kitchen paper, a pair of sharp-ended tweezers, a water pot, narrow double-sided sticky tape, clear silicone glue and some wooden cocktail sticks, a bunch of stamens with tiny heads, a few tiny pearl beads . . . and a lot of patience.

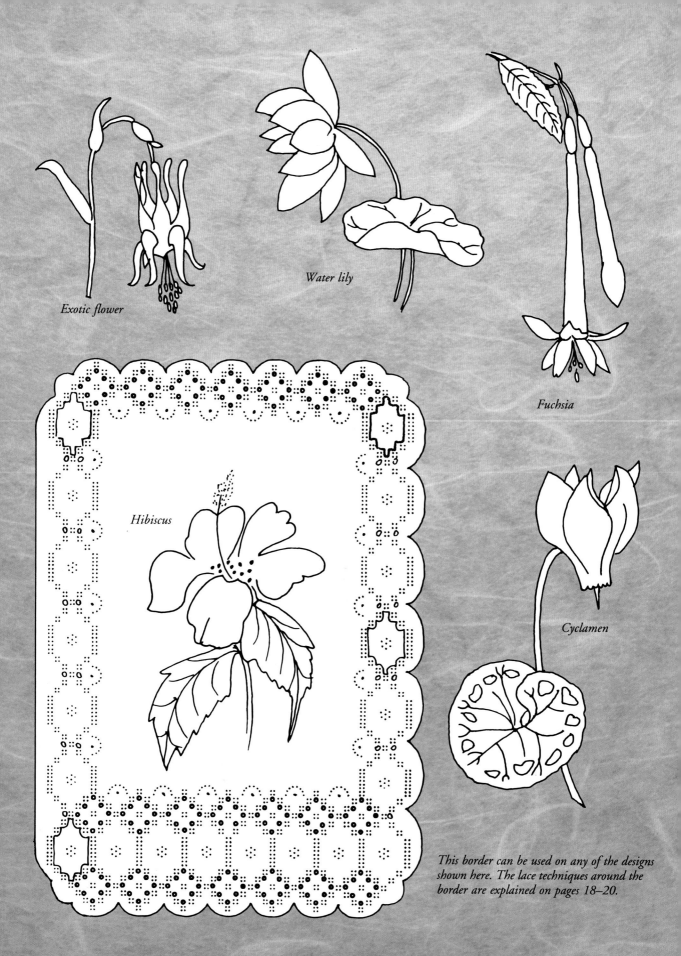

Exotic flower

Water lily

Fuchsia

Hibiscus

Cyclamen

This border can be used on any of the designs shown here. The lace techniques around the border are explained on pages 18–20.

White work

Before you start adding colour, you must first learn the techniques of tracing the design, embossing it and then perforating a lace border. In this section, I have included a practice sheet containing various designs that look good as white images. The practice sheet also includes a border that you can perforate and use to surround all of the designs. For the tracing and embossing exercises I have used the water lily design, and for the perforating exercise, I have used the fuchsia design.

Tools

The exercises in this chapter require the following tools:

Tracing   For white work trace the design with a mapping pen and white acrylic ink. Other colours, especially sepia and antelope brown, are used for coloured images.

A sharp white pencil is useful for tracing continuous fine lines in borders – and it can be erased if you make a mistake.

Embossing   Use a combination of three tools to build up effects: the 4mm plastic-headed tool to warm up the paper and produce soft white effects; then the 3, 1.5 and 1mm steel tools (depending on the effect you want to achieve) to complete the image; and a stylus, which has a sharp point, for embossing very fine lines in borders. You can also use the 3 and 4mm tools to smooth out any lumpy embossing made with the finer tools.

Stippling   I have included a needle tool which, although not essential, I find useful for creating fine texture.

Perforating   For the border given on the practice sheet you need the 1-, 2-, 4- and 7-needle tools and the half-circle needle tool. Use your scissors to cut to crosses and slots. I also illustrate a 3-needle tool used in some of the other borders in this book.

Sharp pointed scissors

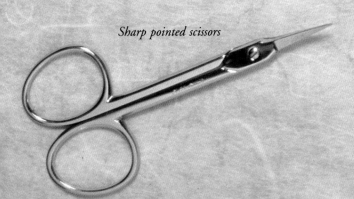

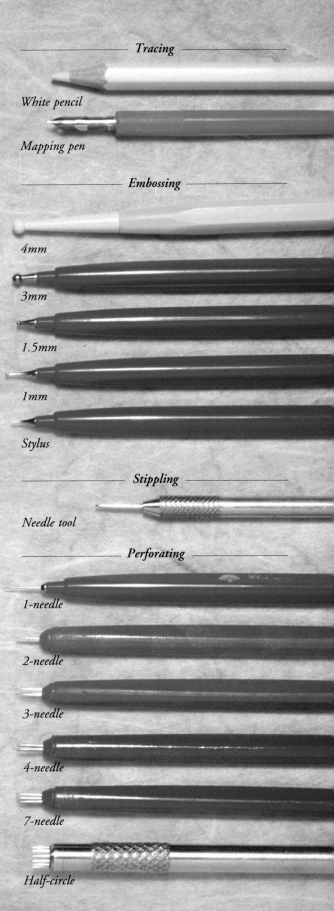

Tracing

White pencil

Mapping pen

Embossing

4mm

3mm

1.5mm

1mm

Stylus

Stippling

Needle tool

Perforating

1-needle

2-needle

3-needle

4-needle

7-needle

Half-circle

Tracing

This simple technique is one of the most important features of parchment craft; you need to have an outlined shape within which to work.

Practise the tracing techniques before you begin, so that you do not spoil your first design. If you have a wobbly hand, it may help to rest it on the embossing pad while tracing.

The traced line must be as fine as possible, and this is governed by the way you hold the pen, not the size of the nib. Dipping a new nib in boiling water will improve its writing qualities. Wipe it dry with kitchen paper before dipping it into the ink.

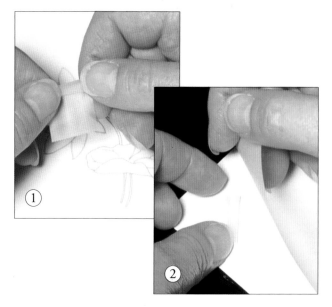

1. Carefully position the parchment paper over the pattern. Roll two small pieces of tape into cylinders, with the sticky sides outermost.

2. Lift the top corner of the parchment paper and, avoiding the design area, place a sticky roll between the pattern and the parchment paper. Press lightly to secure the paper so that it does not slip when you are tracing.

3. Shake the ink well, then fill the nib using the dropper. If you do not have a dropper, simply dip the pen into the ink.

4. Start to trace the design. Hold the pen upright and let it skate across the surface very lightly to get a fine line. The more pressure you apply on the nib, the thicker the line will be.

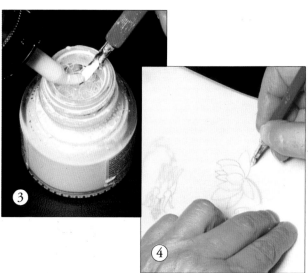

TIP: Keeping your nib clean

- When the nib reservoir empties, wipe the nib on a small sponge soaked in water before dipping it in the ink again. When you have finished tracing, clean the nib and dry it with kitchen paper before putting the pen away.

TIP: Tracing fine lines in borders

- Embossing over an ink-traced line will make the ink go black, and it is also virtually impossible to follow a fine line with an embossing tool. By using a white pencil, you can erase any mistakes with a rubber.

Embossing

Embossing is achieved by rubbing the rounded point of an embossing tool over the surface of a sheet of parchment paper laid on the soft side of an embossing pad. Rubbing causes the fibres of the paper to be displaced and bruised which results in a change of colour – it also makes the paper more elastic, allowing you to increase the pressure and, subsequently, to whiten the colour further.

The more you rub the paper surface, the whiter the result will be. Work from side to side within a traced area; do not go round and round to start with, or you will get a small black mark in the middle of your working area.

Use a selection of tools as an artist uses his colour palette – but instead of painting in colour, use the tools to produce shades of white. In general, the larger the embossing tip, the greyer the effect, and the smaller it is, the whiter the effect.

You can emboss on both side of the paper to produce concave and convex shapes; this will help create depth in your images.

It is important to make sure that you have a balanced visual effect, i.e. not too much white or grey in any one area. The focal point of your finished piece will be the whitest area, so bear this in mind before you begin.

1. Trace the water lily design. Look at the design and decide which parts need concave embossing, and which need convex embossing. For those of you unfamiliar with these terms, look at the two pictures of my hand which show the shapes. Mark the design to show the shapes as shown above – the letter 'A' represents the concave shapes which are embossed from the front, and the letter 'B' the convex ones which are embossed from the back.

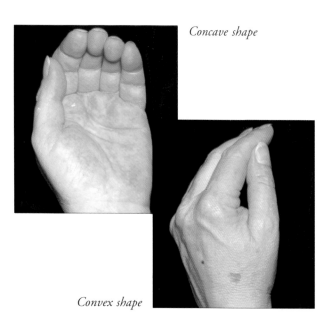

Concave shape

Convex shape

TIP: Embossing

- When embossing remember the shape of the petals. I have seen some flowers that look like flying saucers because they have been embossed too hard from edge to edge.
- Petal edges should sink back into the paper. Emboss the central area of the petal and then soften the embossing as you reach the edges.

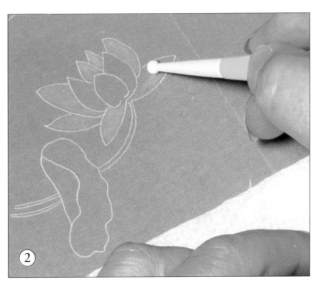

2. Place the parchment paper (with the tracing uppermost) on the soft side of your embossing pad, and a piece of plain paper on which to rest your hands, just below the design. Start embossing with the 4mm plastic tool; its large ball tip is excellent for undercoating and produces a good base grey tone. Rub the area within each petal outline (shape A), working gently from side to side. Exert more pressure each time you rub, until the paper starts to discolour.

3. When all the concave petals have been under-coated, change to the 3mm steel tool and start to whiten the central areas of each petal. Work over the undercoat, carefully embossing selected areas to give shape and form. Do not work over the traced lines with a steel tool, as this will turn them black. Work down the design, keeping the paper firmly in position as you build up the embossing.

TIP: Waxing the embossing tools
Keep a small pot of wax on the work surface when you are embossing your designs and use this to lubricate the tools frequently to keep them smooth. This will lessen any friction between the ball tips and the paper surface when you are rubbing the areas to be embossed.

4. Go back to the 4mm tool and emboss out to the edges of the petals; try to emphasize the curve of each petal by graduating the tones of white.

5. Now change to the stylus and, with its sharp point, accentuate the tips of the petals. Use the stylus like the other embossing tools, working from side to side or up and down to build up white highlights.

6. When you have finished all the concave-shaped petals, turn the parchment paper over and work the convex petals as described in stages 2–5.

7. Without turning the paper over, use the 1.5mm tool to create a lip round the edges of some of the concave petals (shape A). Gradually increase the pressure until the desired effect is achieved.

8. Shape and form can be worked into a chosen area. Here, the main petal is an important part of the design, and to give it form, turn the paper over and emboss a loop shape around the petal edge using the 3mm tool.

The finished design, without a border. Check the front of the design frequently when you are using the different tools, to check your progress as you go along. If the petals look grey, rubbing them harder should produce a white, raised design. Keep working on the shape, form and colour until you are happy with the result.

Stippling fine detail

For the fine markings of the anthers on the long stamen in the hibiscus design, use a stippling tool or a 1-needle tool to create a stippled effect. Place the design on a piece of strong card and move the tool up and down with small rapid movements, puncturing the paper with a series of small dots. This is a useful technique that can be used for the centres of lots of other flowers.

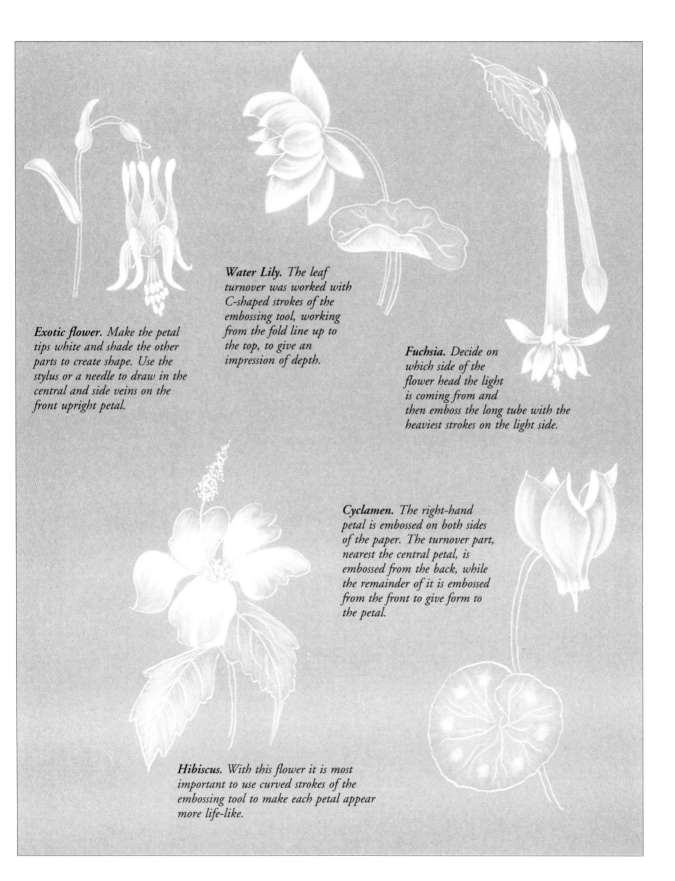

Exotic flower. *Make the petal tips white and shade the other parts to create shape. Use the stylus or a needle to draw in the central and side veins on the front upright petal.*

Water Lily. *The leaf turnover was worked with C-shaped strokes of the embossing tool, working from the fold line up to the top, to give an impression of depth.*

Fuchsia. *Decide on which side of the flower head the light is coming from and then emboss the long tube with the heaviest strokes on the light side.*

Cyclamen. *The right-hand petal is embossed on both sides of the paper. The turnover part, nearest the central petal, is embossed from the back, while the remainder of it is embossed from the front to give form to the petal.*

Hibiscus. *With this flower it is most important to use curved strokes of the embossing tool to make each petal appear more life-like.*

Perforating

When you are happy with your tracing and embossing skills try creating a border round the design using the technique of perforating. Lace grid patterns are the foundation of delicate lace-like borders. For this exercise I use the fuchsia design to fill the central space but any of the designs given on the practice sheet will fit.

TIP: Using lace grid patterns

Lace grid patterns can only be used twice before they are destroyed by the perforations, so I suggest photocopying them before you start.

1. Look at the design and decide on the tools you will need. I have annotated a detail of the border pattern used in this exercise to show those needed here.

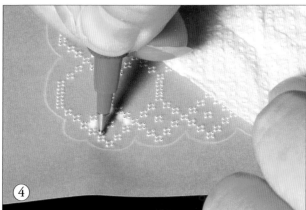

2. Secure the parchment over the pattern (see page 12) and then use a white pencil to trace the scalloped border.

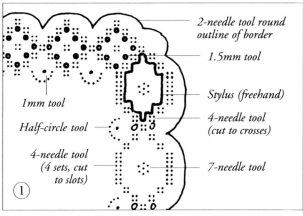

3. Using the 4-needle tool, mark the four-point lace grid. Marking is a partial perforation – the needles should only just break through the paper. Trace the fuchsia design in the middle with a mapping pen and white ink.

4. Remove the paper from the pattern, turn it over and place it on your embossing pad. Emboss the fuchsia and then the sets of eight small circles in the border design with the 1.5mm tool.

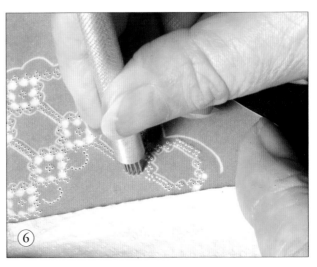

5. Following the traced white pencil line, emboss the scalloped, outside edge of the border with the stylus. Next, use the same tool freehand to draw in the small panels within the lace pattern. The sharp point of the stylus will give a fine white line, creating a delicate embossed effect on the finished design.

6. Still working on the back of the parchment paper, use the half-circle needle tool to complete the inside edges of the border. Working from the back adds texture to the front of the design.

7. Change to the 7-needle tool and perforate the circles in the centre of each small panel, again working from the back to the front.

8. Re-perforate the whole lace grid border with the 4-needle tool to make the holes bigger. Turn the paper over and re-perforate the half-circle and 7-needle tool work as well.

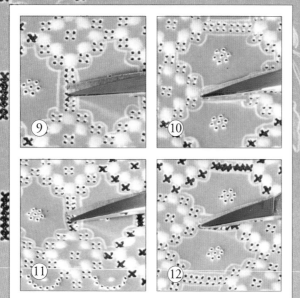

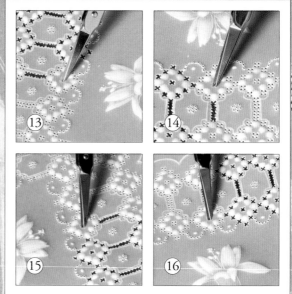

9–12. Using sharp, pointed scissors, cut the 4-needle grid to slots. Insert the tips of the scissors between the first two holes in the long side of a slot area and snip the gap. Work down this side (9), across the top (10), down the other side (11), and finally snip the gap between the two holes at the other end (12).

13–16. Now use a similar action to cut the remaining 4-needle grid to crosses. Snip between two holes on one side of the square (13), turn the paper through 90° and snip between the two holes on the next side (14), turn the paper again and snip the third side (15), and finally turn it once more and snip the fourth side (16).

Finishing off the card

You can simply fold the embossed parchment paper to make it into a card but you can also make the card more interesting by sewing in a coloured insert.

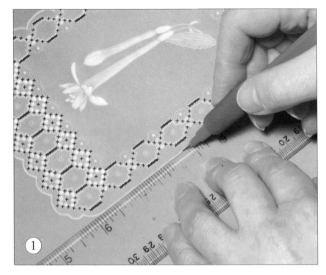

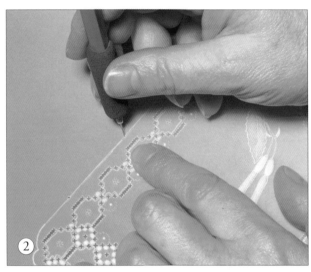

1. Working on the back of the design, use a ruler and the stylus tool to gently emboss the fold line.

2. Turn the embossed design over and place a suitable insert paper underneath. Starting at the middle of the fold line, use the 1-needle tool to pierce three evenly-spaced holes along the fold line.

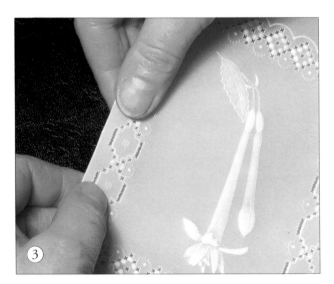

3. Separate the two sheets of paper and fold them so that the three holes stay on the fold line. Define the fold edge on the parchment paper by gently pinching it between fingers and thumbs.

4. Thread a needle with decorative thread. From the inside, pass the needle out through the middle hole, in through the bottom one, out through the top one and then back through the middle hole. Tie a neat knot on the inside.

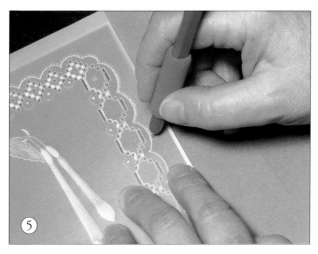

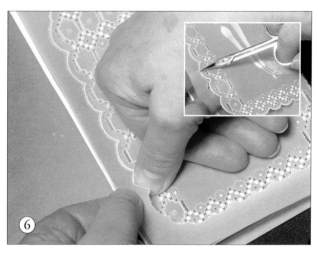

5. Using the 2-needle tool, perforate round the outside edge of the card taking the points through all four layers of paper.

6. Press a thumbnail over the perforated edge and gently strip off the outside of the top layer of paper. Cut away parts that do not tear easily. Finish by tearing away the outside pieces of the other three layers.

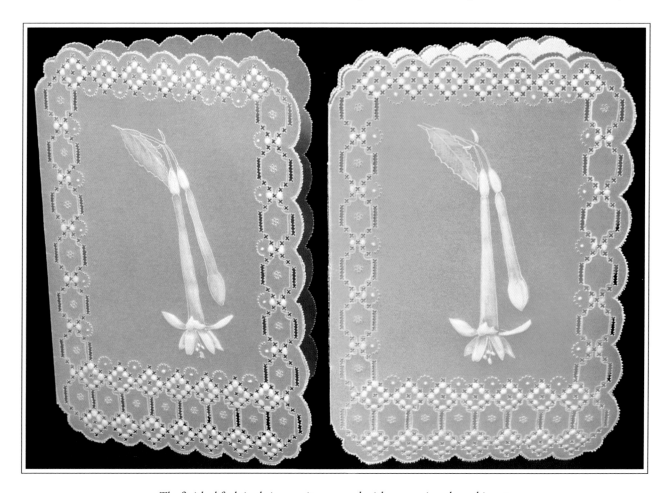

The finished fuchsia design, on its own and with a sewn-in coloured insert.

Here is the hibiscus embossed within the border design and made into a card with a graduated paper insert. Note that the whitest parts are the curves on the petals which catch the light. Different coloured inserts produce a variety of effects and I suggest you try several colours behind one image to see the differences. When buying paper for inserts, take a piece of parchment paper with you because the colours will look completely different behind it.

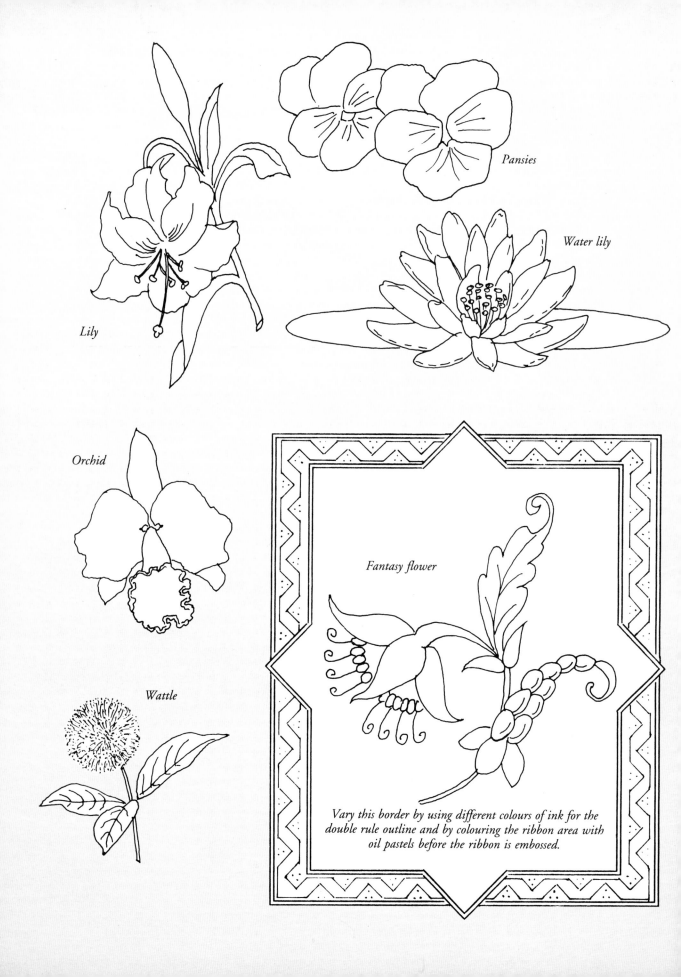

Pansies

Water lily

Lily

Orchid

Fantasy flower

Wattle

Vary this border by using different colours of ink for the double rule outline and by colouring the ribbon area with oil pastels before the ribbon is embossed.

Using oil pastels and watercolour pencils

Oil pastel and watercolour pencil colouring is the simplest method of adding colour, and it is also my favourite technique. Beautiful effects can be achieved easily and carefully chosen colours will complement delicate lace borders and white embossed designs. In this chapter I show you how to use oil pastels and watercolour pencils, and a border which is traced with gold acrylic ink is also included. The fantasy flower pattern is used to show the technique of colouring with oil pastels.

Materials

Oil pastels   There are many brands of oil pastels available and it is advisable to buy a box that contains four or five shades of each colour. Reds, blues, yellows and greens are ideal for flower designs, and darker shades are useful when building up layers of colour. Some oil pastels tend to crumble during the colouring process, resulting in a powdery residue falling on to your work – keep some paper on your work surface, away from your parchment design, and regularly tap the design on it to remove the excess oil pastel.

Blend the oil pastel colours into each other with a small amount of medium. Everyone has their own favourite medium – I use a colourless barbecue igniter, which is virtually odour-free, but you can also use white spirit. Make sure you work in an well-ventilated room and do not smoke.

Pearlised oil pastels are available in a good range of colours. I apply them to the design after the embossing process, using a piece of dry kitchen paper or the tip of my finger. Unlike other oil pastels, they are not spread with a medium. I have used pearlised oil pastels on the petals of the water lily (see page 31).

Watercolour pencils   I use these with oil pastels to add shape and form. I work the darker shades of the pencils into the coloured design to add depth and tone and to give a more realistic, three-dimensional feel to the image. There are many makes of watercolour pencil, all with different qualities, so try some out before purchasing a whole set.

Acrylic inks   When using oil pastels I trace the pattern with antelope brown or sepia ink. The traced lines then blend into the colours in the main design, complementing shades and tones.

I also use gold ink for decoration. The technique for tracing with gold ink is slightly different to the method shown on page 12. I use a steel-nibbed pen, and stir up the ink before filling the reservoir. This ensures that the suspension mixes with the gold powder. The effects of this ink on white and coloured designs are lovely. Borders, edges and images are enhanced, even with just a tiny touch of gold.

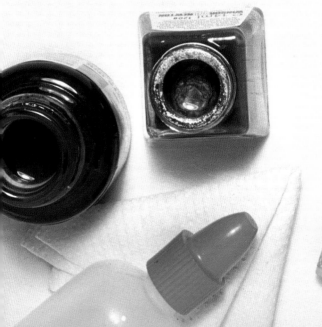

Colouring the design

First, trace the fantasy flower design on to the parchment, using antelope brown or sepia acrylic ink.

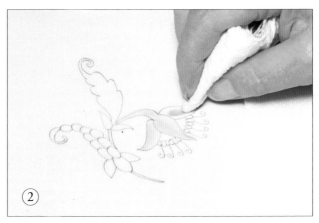

1. Choose three shades of the same colour for the main petals. Turn the paper over to the wrong side and apply the middle shade to the petal centres.

2. Fold a sheet of kitchen paper diagonally into four to make a point. Moisten the tip with medium and work the colour to the outer edges of the petals.

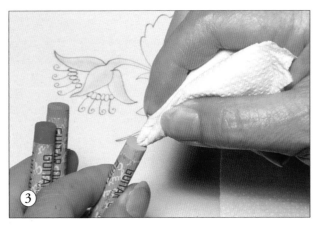

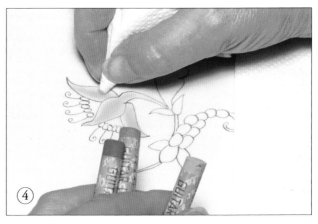

3. Turn the paper to the right side. Using the tip of the kitchen paper moistened with medium, apply the palest shade in areas that catch the light. Work carefully, blending the colour towards the outside edges.

4. Apply the darkest shade, gently blending the two colours together, increasing the intensity of colour and adding form.

TIP: Applying oil pastels

- For an even colour, use clean, dry kitchen paper to remove excess medium and oil pastel.
- Wipe away mistakes with clean kitchen paper moistened with medium.

- For small areas, take the colour from the pastel with the paper point and apply to the design.
- Make a new point on the kitchen paper for each colour you use.

(5)

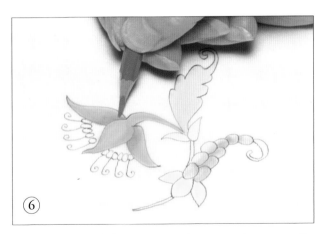

(6)

5. Fill in the rest of the flower with the oil pastels. To make it more realistic, and to give an impression of depth and form, add shading.

6. Work the darker areas with watercolour pencils. Choose colours to complement the oil pastels already used. Work over the base colour, lightly feathering the edge of the petals to create depth.

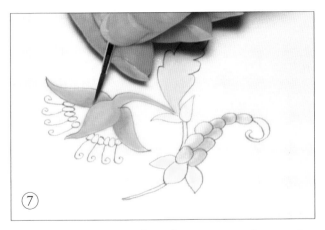

(7)

(8)

7. Gently paint into the colour using a damp paint brush to add definition. Spread the colour out into the petals, deepening the tones on the tips and edges.

8. Continue in the same way on the other areas of the design until you have completed the whole flower.

TIP: Using watercolour pencils

- Sharpen watercolour pencils with a craft knife. Pencil sharpeners will break their fragile leads.
- To erase lines where the colour has been applied too vigorously, simply blend the colours using clean kitchen paper moistened with medium.
- Do not take the colour from the tip of the watercolour pencils with a wet paint brush. The water may leak from the brush into the pencil and destroy the lead.

- Use a shader brush (a small flat brush) for shading and deepening tones.
- Always apply the pencil to the paper first, then work over the area with a wet brush.
- Use tiny, circular brush strokes within the traced lines. This produces a lovely shaded area which will blend into the background colours.
- Practise the techniques on a spare piece of paper before colouring your design.

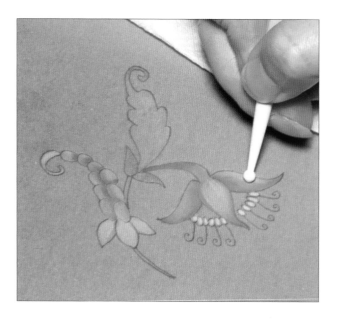

Embossing the design

Embossing an oil pastel design is entirely different to embossing a white or painted pattern. The aim is to achieve texture, not a raised effect. Both sides of the design can be embossed. Turn the design over as you work to check the effects you are getting. It is useful to observe flowers, and to aquaint yourself with the shapes and characteristics of petals, stems and leaves.

The larger embossing heads (4mm and 3mm) give the best results working over oil pastel and watercolour pencil, and the plastic 4mm tool does not leave silvery marks on the surface of the paper. For tiny areas, where petals fold over for example, emboss very gently with the 1.5mm tool. Add veins and fine lines with a 1-needle tool or a stylus on the front of the parchment paper.

With all the embossing tools, gently work over the colour, rubbing the tool from side to side. The paper will take on a textured appearance.

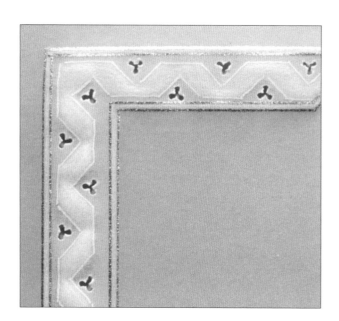

Border design

Place the flower over the border pattern. Draw in the card edges and fold line using white pencil. Trace the border outline with gold ink (see tip below), and the ribbon pattern with white ink.

Using oil pastels, colour the enclosed border area on the back of the paper. Emboss the ribbon first with the 3mm tool to warm up the paper, then with the 1.5mm tool to whiten the design.

> **TIP: Using metallic inks**
>
> Use a steel-nibbed pen for metallic inks – the bowl is larger and holds the weight of metallic ink better than a small mapping nib. If you get a blot, place the edge of a piece of kitchen paper against the blot; when the paper stops absorbing, move to a clean area. Once you have removed most of the excess ink, dab the area with clean pieces of kitchen paper until you are left with a faint gold tinge. Let this dry completely and then gently rub with a soft eraser. You may not be able to get rid of it completely but most of it will disappear.

The lace effect on this border is made with a 3-needle tool. Follow the pattern and mark the surface of the paper with the tool all round the border. You can use the cut-to-crosses technique (see page 20) to make small star shapes as shown in the left of inset opposite. However, if, while the 3-needle tool is fully down, you twist it slightly to the left and right you will create slots rather than holes; these can either be left as they are or cut to make larger shamrock shapes.

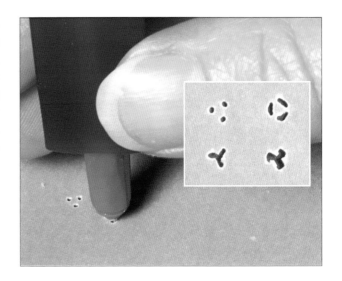

The finished fantasy flower card

Pansies. Draw the lines on the flower centres with dry watercolour pencils over the oil pastel base. Keep the lines close together and work from the centre outwards to get a random-edged effect.

Lily. Emboss the central vein on each leaf from the front. Keep the dots of colour on the petals small – use a watercolour pencil or apply sepia ink with a spotter brush.

Water lily. Use pearlised oil pastels on the petals to create a translucent effect, and plain oil pastels on the leaf pad. Highlight the centre of the lily with gold acrylic inks.

Orchid. Emboss the trumpet and the frilled edge of the throat from the back of the paper. Do not emboss the petals right up to their edges.

Fantasy flower. Draw the lines in the flower centres with dry water-colour pencils over an oil pastel base. Keep the lines close together and work outwards from the centre.

Wattle. Use a stylus tool to stipple over an oil pastel base on the head of this flower, and then a 1-needle tool to create the hair-like stems on the puff ball.

Pearlised oil pastels

Pearlised oil pastels produce a sheen that can be used to good effect on the wax-like petals of plants such as water lilies and orchids.

In this example, I traced the petals with white ink and used the white work embossing techniques (see pages 12–15) to produce a life-like flower. I then wiped a tiny amount of pink pearlised oil pastel over the front of the petals to create a hint of colour.

Water lilies do come in a variety of colours, so you can colour them with ordinary oil pastels and, when you have finished embossing them, use pearlised oil pastels to create a realistic finish. A good gardening book, especially one with painted illustrations rather than photographs, will prove a wonderful reference source.

Wiping a tiny amount of pearlised oil pastel over white work will add realism to the wax-like petals of the water lily.

The finished water lily design in the ribbon border. I created the effect of water in the foreground by blending sea green and blue oil pastels and colouring the area under the lily pad.

Morning glory card

The flower is cut out so that it overlaps the background. Trace the card edges, and the central and middle fold line, with a white pencil, then trace the flower using sepia ink.

Colouring the design

Colour the flower first, beginning on the back of the design. Using oil pastels, choose two shades of blue and green and apply the darker shades to the petals and leaves. Turn the design over and apply the two colours, working from the palest to the darkest. More definition is required where the petals overlap so

blend in blue watercolour pencil, to deepen the tones. Mark the veins on the leaves with a brown watercolour pencil. Finally add yellow oil pastel to the flower centres.

Embossing the design

Using the plastic headed tool, gently emboss the flower petals in the lightest areas. This will give the petals a slight curve upwards. Turn the design over and use the 1.5mm tool to emboss the yellow centres. Finally, run a line down the centre of each leaf with a 1-needle tool.

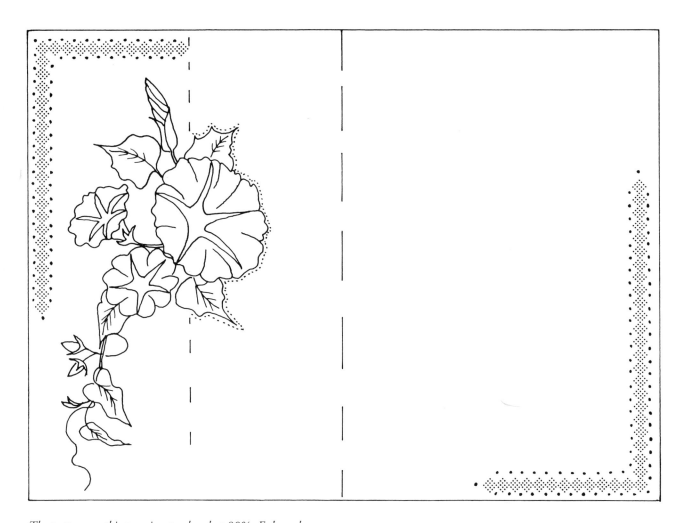

The pattern on this page is reproduced at 80%. Enlarge by 125% to get a full-size pattern.

Border design

The lace grid round the border forms a diamond pattern. Using the 4-needle tool, gently mark the design on the front of the paper (see Stage 3 on page 18). Working from the back of the picture, emboss the small dots in the lace grid using the stylus.

From the front of the design, re-perforate the 4-needle grid, then cut the central part of each diamond to crosses. Cut around the edge of the card with scissors, then carefully perforate the lines around the overlapping flower and leaves using a single needle tool. Gently cut these perforations with scissors.

On the front of the design, emboss the central fold line with the stylus. Turn the design over and emboss the two short fold lines on the front. Fold the front page back leaving the main flower and leaves flat, then fold the central line inwards to form the card.

The finished card.

Art nouveau lady

Colouring faces is always a problem and many of us, I am sure, will have produced a face that looks as though the subject has a nasty skin problem or needs eye surgery! Here is how to avoid that happening.

Colouring and embossing

Trace flesh outlines, features and hair with sepia ink – black always looks too heavy. Eyebrows are a series of fine lines at a slight angle and lashes are angled towards the outer corner of the eye. Do not emphasize lower lashes; a few very short ones at the outer eye corner edge is enough.

Trace the irises with blue, dark green or brown ink, and remember that they are not completely round as the eyelids hide the top and bottom curves. Use a brush and the same colour ink to fill in each iris. Draw the pupils with black ink and fill them in with a brush. Using a pen, add a highlight dot of white ink to the iris of each eye making sure that it is in the same position in both eyes. Emboss the white of the eye area from the back of the paper.

Use a thin wash of ink (pinky-red, not a vivid shade) to colour the lips and a pale brown oil pastel on the back of the paper for the flesh areas. Add shadows to the face and neck, and a faint blush to the cheeks, using oil pastel on the front of the paper.

For the hair, choose three shades of oil pastel – remember that blondes and redheads both have some brown in their hair. Spread the middle colour oil pastel on the back of the paper, and then use the shading techniques (see page 26) on the front to produce realistic hair. Lightly emboss for texture and add fine flecks with a stylus to give highlights.

The pattern on this page is reproduced at 80%. Enlarge by 125% to get a full-size pattern.

For the dress, a mixture of techniques have been used. The white areas are advanced embossing techniques, whilst the jewelled pectoral uses gold ink tracing and felt-tip techniques. The flowers in the hair are pearlised ink and the centres are produced by using bead point (a special material used for painting cross stitch type patterns). Bead point work must be left to dry for at least twenty-four hours.

Working the border

Using gold ink, trace the edges of the card and the double-circle border. Emboss the space between the circles or fill it with oil pastel. Mark the lace grid, emboss the design in the border, re-perforate the lace and cut to crosses.

Two versions of the finished picture. On the upper one, I traced the two circles with white ink and coloured the gap between. On the lower one, I coloured the border area between the outer gold circle and the outside edge with a pale blue oil pastel and embossed the gap between the two circles.

Water nymph

Convolvulus

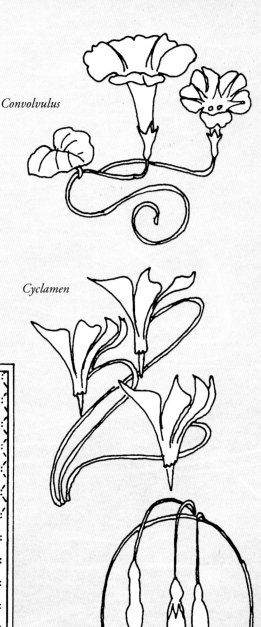

Cyclamen

Azalea

Fuchsia

Using felt-tip pens

Felt-tip pens are so easy to use and they are readily available in a wonderful range of colours. Vibrant shades can be mixed and matched to complement delicate patterns, and a wide range of tones can be achieved simply by painting over colours with a paintbrush. The full-size patterns opposite are all suitable for use with felt-tip pens, and they will all fit within the border design; for the colouring exercise in this chapter the fuchsia design is used.

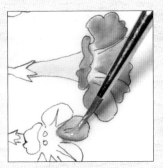

Make a thin wash of interference medium and use it to spread the felt-tip colour and create an opalescent finish to your work. You can also apply a thin wash of interence medium over white embossed areas such as the lilies in the hair of the water nymph.

Materials

Felt-tip pens   I usually use cheap water-based felt-tips which can be bought in plastic packs containing up to thirty-six different colours and which give you two or three shades of the same colour.

Tracing ink   Trace with black ink (it does not seem to look right if you trace in any other colour).

Interference medium   This is a medium which gives an opalescent tinge to felt-tip colours. It is readily available in several shades and can be mixed with water to produce a thin wash.

Colouring with felt-tip pens

Trace the design on to the parchment paper using a mapping pen and black ink to outline the flower; the strong colours produced by felt-tip pens contrast well with the darker outlines.

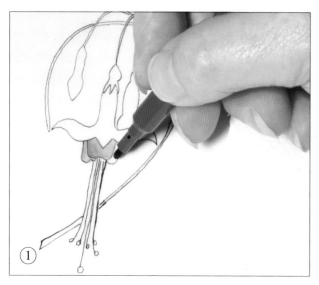

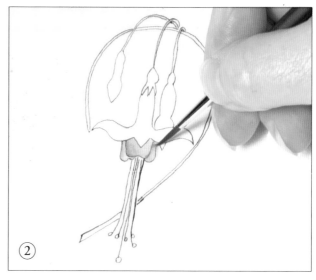

1. Gently apply purple to the flower centre, keeping within the traced outline.

2. Carefully blend the colour from the centre outwards using a brush moistened with a little water.

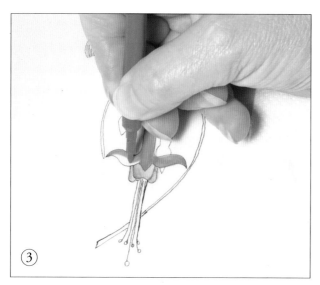

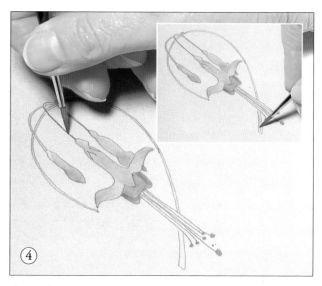

3. Choose a bright red and stroke the colour on to the bell-shaped cap in overlapping stripes. Keep within the outlines and do not go over into the purple flower centre.

4. Colour the flower stems with green, taking the colour from the tip of a felt-tip pen with a paint brush. Paint the main stem with a blend of brown and green to make a more life-like image.

Embossing the design

Parchment paper is non-absorbant, so make sure your work is dry before starting to emboss it. The colours will become more vibrant as you work, so check your progress regularly.

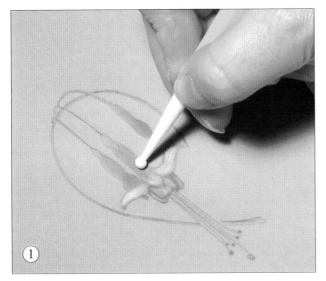

1. All of this design is embossed from the back. Start with the 4mm plastic tool on the tube and sepals.

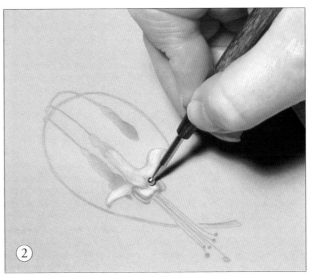

2. Use the 3mm tool on the front petal, the seed heads and the large stem.

3. Finally, emboss the stamens using the 1mm tool.

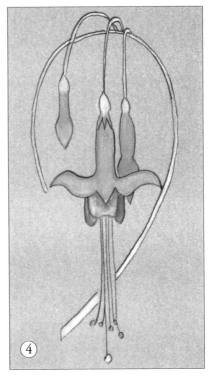

The finished fuchsia, coloured with felt-tip pens and embossed.

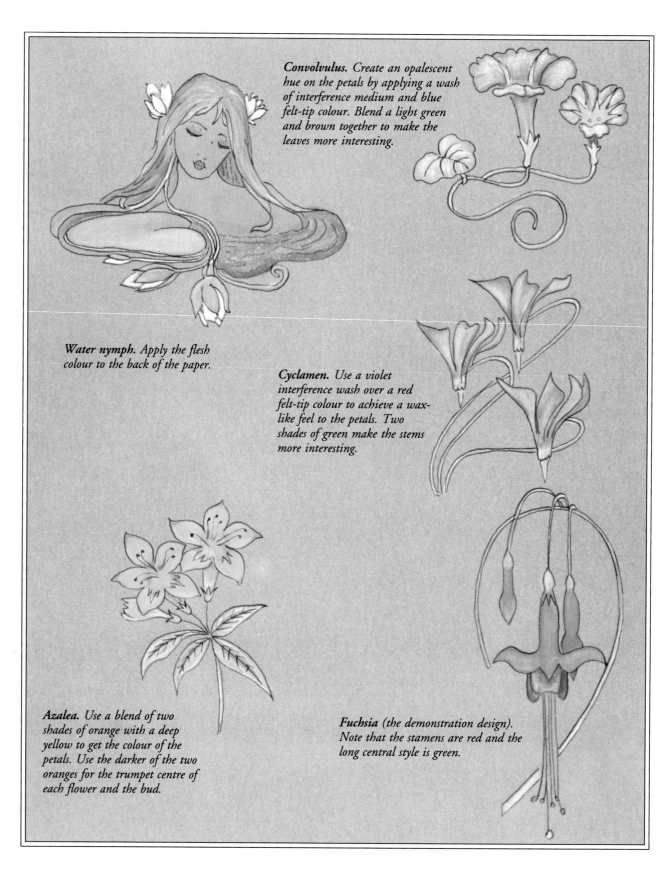

Convolvulus. Create an opalescent hue on the petals by applying a wash of interference medium and blue felt-tip colour. Blend a light green and brown together to make the leaves more interesting.

Water nymph. Apply the flesh colour to the back of the paper.

Cyclamen. Use a violet interference wash over a red felt-tip colour to achieve a wax-like feel to the petals. Two shades of green make the stems more interesting.

Azalea. Use a blend of two shades of orange with a deep yellow to get the colour of the petals. Use the darker of the two oranges for the trumpet centre of each flower and the bud.

Fuchsia (the demonstration design). Note that the stamens are red and the long central style is green.

Border design

The border given on the worksheet can be used with any of the other images – some of them will need a portrait layout while others, such as the water nymph illustrated below, need a landscape one.

Trace the double-rule outer border and the double ovals with gold ink, then fill the oval using gold ink and a paint brush. Mark the lace grid with the 4-needle tool.

Emboss the short straight lines in the lace grid with a 1-needle tool and a ruler, and the gap between the double-rule outer border and the oval with the 3mm tool.

Re-perforate the lace grid and cut to crosses. Finish the card by cutting the straight edges to size.

Pearlised inks can be mixed with water and used to spread colours. The effect is gently pearlescent when embossed.

On this version of the border design the centre of the oval has been perforated and cut out to reveal the water nymph on the inside. Do not be afraid of experimenting with different colourways – as you can see from the three images on these pages, it is impossible to replicate a design even with the same set of colours.

Mandarin ducks

In China, Mandarin ducks symbolise conjugal fidelity and are often given as wedding presents so it would be appropriate to use this as a wedding card.

Begin by marking the outside edge of the card and the fold line with a white pencil and then trace the central design using black ink.

Colouring and embossing the design

Use cobalt blue oil pastel for the sky area and Prussian blue for the water area. Add colour to the ducks with felt-tips and spread with a damp brush. Use dark blue for the crests; pale pink for the neck feathers; a mixture of dark blue and green for the backs; grey for the chests; yellow for the upright wings; red for the bills; rust for the tails; and pale pink for the underbellies. Add colour to the foliage: use grey-green for the bamboo grass and dark green for the leaves on the water. Emboss the ducks, grasses and leaves.

Full-size pattern.

The finished Mandarin ducks card.

Border design

Use gold ink for the double border lines (both square and scalloped) and the flowers in the lace grid. Fill in the double outlines of the scalloped central border using a paint brush and gold ink. Mark the lace grid.

Emboss the petals and the dots in the lace grid and the double border areas (both square and scalloped). Re-perforate the lace grid and cut to crosses. Finally, cut the edges of the card straight.

43

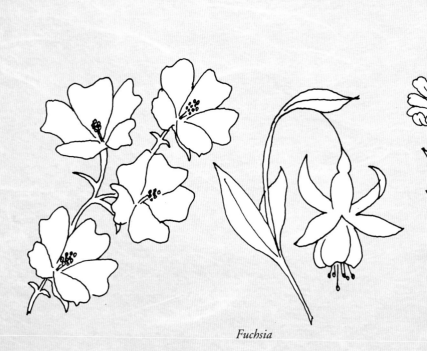

Daisy

Fuchsia

Mallow

Pansies

Fantasy flower

Snake head fritillary

Using inks

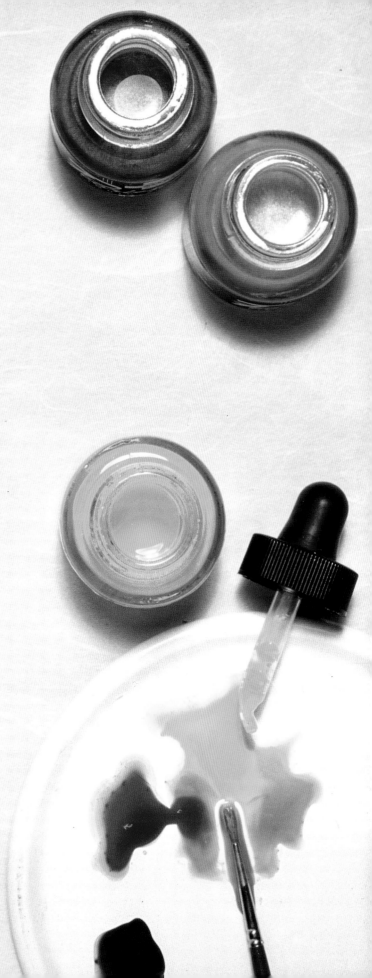

Lovely delicate results can be achieved with inks, and they can be mixed with water to create almost transparent washes. Trace flower outlines in the colours they are going to be painted with. If a flower has a white petal then it will not require painting – simply trace in white and then emboss.

Again, I have selected a set of full-size patterns that lend themselves to being coloured with inks. The fritillary is used as the example in this chapter.

Materials

Acrylic inks   It is best to use inks with a stable pigmentation to ensure good results. Clearer and more delicate colours can be created with properly pigmented inks and they can be mixed together to obtain different shades. I use acrylic inks which are available in many different colours.

Pearlised inks   These are very easy to use and I love the soft effects that can be created with them. Usually their colours are so delicate that they can be used directly from the palette.

Colouring the design

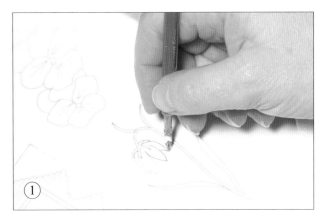

1. Using a pen, trace the flower head with purple lake, and the leaves and stems with olive green.

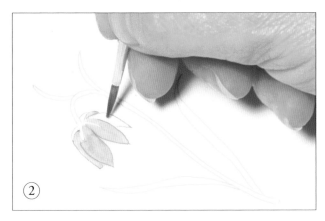

2. Apply a thin wash of purple lake to the petals.

3. When dry, use a pen to draw the lines that extend from the top to the bottom of the petal.

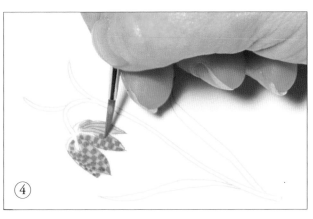

4. Using undiluted purple lake, add the chequered effect that is unique to this flower.

TIP: Using inks

- Use the side of the brush to lay washes into large areas and the tip for smaller ones.
- Apply wet over dry washes to build up extra colour where you need it. Once the base coat is dry, it acts as a waterproof base for the colours.
- Use undiluted ink, applied with a pen or brush, to add stamens and other details.

5. Make a thin wash of olive green and use this to paint the stems and leaves.

6. Mix some antelope brown to the wash and use this to paint one side of each of the two large leaves.

7. With a pen and undiluted olive green ink, draw in the central veins of the two large leaves.

Embossing the design

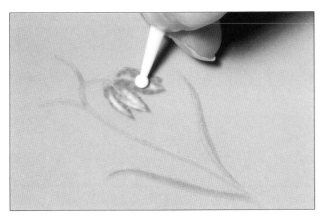

Emboss the central area of the petals using the plastic 4mm tool. Emboss each petal of the fritillary and one side of each of the two large leaves.

The finished snake head fritillary, coloured with inks and embossed.

Border design

Using a white pencil, draw in the card edges and the fold lines around the coloured image, and then mark the corners of the outer double border. Mark the lace grid with a 4-needle tool.

Set a ruler against two corner marks and emboss the outer double border line with a stylus tool. Emboss the curved lines round the lace grid with a stylus.

Re-perforate the lace grid, remembering with this type of grid to let the needle travel only about two thirds of its length. With the single needle tool, perforate holes along the inner double border line, starting with the corners. Try to keep the holes as evenly spaced as possible and make sure the needle travels its full length this time. Cut to crosses each of the outer edge 4-needle perforations and then cut to crosses each alternate 4-needle set of holes.

This snakes head fritillary makes a stunningly simple and elegant card. Carefully select the colour of the paper insert and sew it in with gold thread; in this example, I used a deep fuchsia colour.

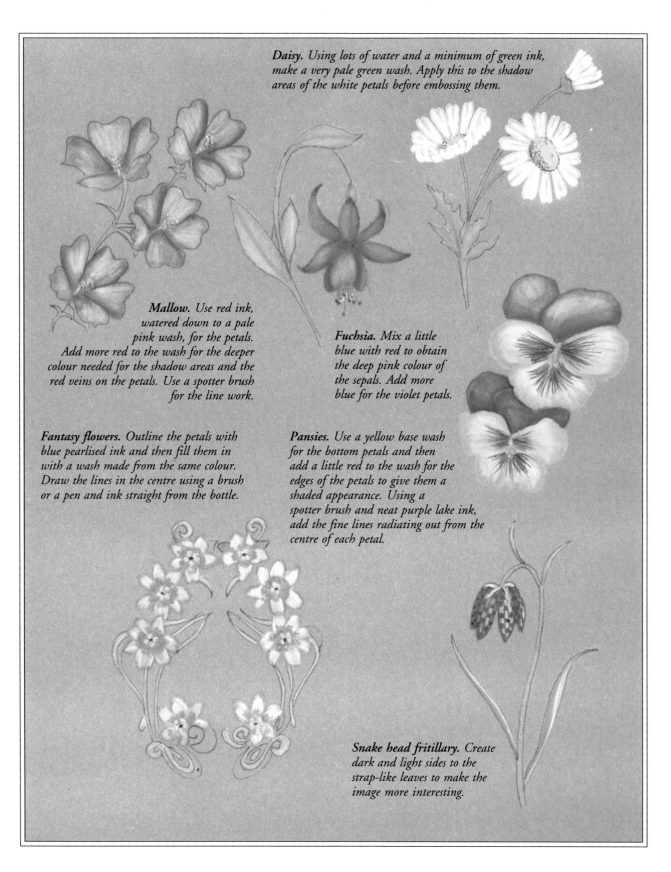

Daisy. Using lots of water and a minimum of green ink, make a very pale green wash. Apply this to the shadow areas of the white petals before embossing them.

Mallow. Use red ink, watered down to a pale pink wash, for the petals. Add more red to the wash for the deeper colour needed for the shadow areas and the red veins on the petals. Use a spotter brush for the line work.

Fuchsia. Mix a little blue with red to obtain the deep pink colour of the sepals. Add more blue for the violet petals.

Fantasy flowers. Outline the petals with blue pearlised ink and then fill them in with a wash made from the same colour. Draw the lines in the centre using a brush or a pen and ink straight from the bottle.

Pansies. Use a yellow base wash for the bottom petals and then add a little red to the wash for the edges of the petals to give them a shaded appearance. Using a spotter brush and neat purple lake ink, add the fine lines radiating out from the centre of each petal.

Snake head fritillary. Create dark and light sides to the strap-like leaves to make the image more interesting.

49

Medieval card

This design could be used as a picture or a card. You can add a name or a greeting in the central scroll if you wish.

Colouring

Trace the network of stems and the outline of the scroll and then, using a brush and gold ink, fill in the stems. Mix a wash of olive green and black for the leaves and olive green and blue for the turnover areas. Paint the leaves and then outline them with a pen and olive green ink.

Paint the little daisy-like flowers red, and use a diluted mixture of red and a little blue on the petals.

Paint the centres of the flowers yellow and gold. Paint the crocus-like flowers with a mixture of well-diluted red and white ink. Using a pen, outline all the flowers with gold ink. Using buff oil pastel on the back of the paper, colour the area bordered by the stems.

Embossing and perforating

Mark the 3-needle lace grid. Emboss the flower petals, the stems, the turnover area of leaves and the design in the lace grid. Re-perforate the 3-needle grid, turning the tool slightly to produce slots and cut to shamrock shapes (see page 29). Fold the card, sew in an insert and cut the sides straight.

These patterns are reproduced at 80%. Enlarge by 125% to get full-size patterns. The narrow pattern is for the book mark on page 5.

The finished card. The bookmark shown on page 5 complements this card and is made using the same techniques.

Islamic card

Using lots of shades of a single colour is very effective on parchment paper. Blue (always a favourite of parchment crafters) has been used for this card but it would look just as good in sepia, green or maroon.

Colouring

Mark the card edges and the fold line with white pencil. Trace the whole design in blue ink and paint the circles in the lace grid with pearlised Dutch blue ink. For the rest of the design, water down your ink on the working palette and paint the flowers, leaves, the inner double border, and within the two inner lines of the outer border. You now have a base to work on. If your ink is not heavily pigmented you may have to add another colour wash to achieve a suitable base.

Use undiluted ink to add darker areas. If you are using lightly pigmented ink you may have to use acrylic paint (watered down on the working palette) to add these details. Keep adding coats of ink until you are happy with the dark areas.

Embossing and perforating

Perforate the lace grid. Emboss the painted border areas, the flowers and some of the leaves to taste. Emboss the design in the lace grid and the painted areas of the lace grid. Re-perforate the lace grid and cut to slots and crosses. Piercing the central area of each pearlised flower in the grid is optional.

Sew in an insert of your choice, fold the card and cut the edges straight.

Full-size pattern.

The finished Islamic card painted in shades of Dutch blue ink. It would look equally good in shades of another colour.

Victorian fan card

This is a very special card, reminiscent of the lovely cards of the Victorian era. You can send it folded so that the recipient can fan it out, or you could affix it to a card with silicone glue already fanned out – the choice is yours. You will need to make six fan vanes.

Colouring

Only pearlised inks are used on this project. Trace the flower petals in violet and then fill them in with a brush. Paint the centres of the flowers and the middle of the embossed petals in the lace grid with yellow. Trace and then fill in the leaves with green and then use bronze for the edges of the lace grid area.

Embossing and perforating

Mark the lace grid. Emboss the flower petals with the 1.5mm tool working from the outside edge towards the centre in overlapping strokes. This will mean that the petal edges are slightly raised but the centres remain untouched. Use the stippling technique for the flower centres. Emboss each leaf lightly from the edge towards the central vein and work at an angle to give texture. Emboss the pointed tips with the 1mm tool. From the front of the paper, draw in the veining with the single needle tool. Emboss the design in the lace grid and use the single needle tool and a ruler to draw in the crisscrossed lines.

Re-perforate and cut to slots and crosses, then perforate out each vane.

Punch a hole in the bottom of each vane as indicated on the pattern. Use an eyelet tool to fix the bottom of the fan together, or thread a piece of ribbon through the bottom hole.

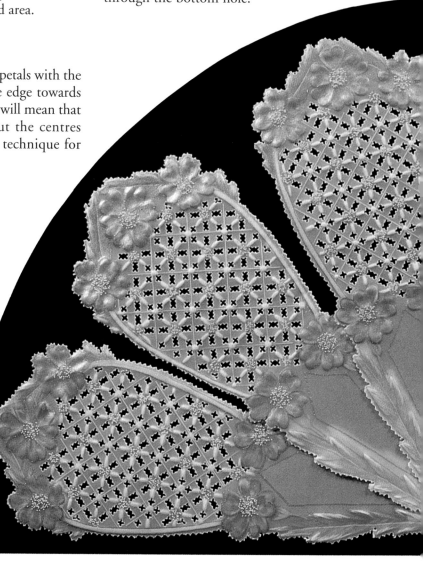

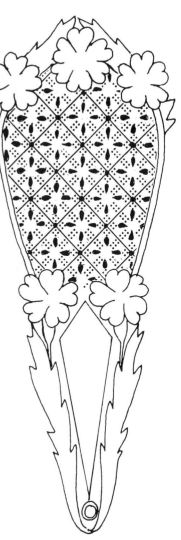

Full-size pattern for fan segment. You will need to make six segments.

The finished fan. You could make the fan more personal by including a short message embossed in the small areas of the segments enclosed within the gold border.

Photograph mount

This pretty mount, in which you can frame your favourite photograph, is coloured with pearlised and acrylic inks.

Colouring

Mark the outer edge of the frame with white pencil. Trace the double outlines of the entwined stems and the bottom of the flowers with gold ink, and the stamens with sepia or antelope brown.

Colour the rest of the design with pearlised inks. Use moon violet to trace and fill in the two large petals on both sides of the central petal of all flowers; sundown magenta for the central and two small outer petals on each flower; a spot of mazuma gold for the anthers at the top of each stamen; and silver moss for the leaves and calyx (inside the gold outline).

The pattern on this page is reproduced at 80%. Enlarge by 125% to get a full-size pattern.

Embossing and perforating

Mark the lace grid. Emboss the double outlines of the stems and the flower petals, calyx and anthers. Emboss the leaves, working from the outside edge to the central vein on each side so that you end up with a thin line down the centre of each leaf that is not embossed. Re-perforate the lace grid and cut to crosses. Secure a piece of coloured paper on the back of the mount with small pieces of double-sided tape (or silicone glue) behind embossed pieces of the design. Perforate out the central area of the frame, going through both layers of paper, and cut round the outer edge of the mount.

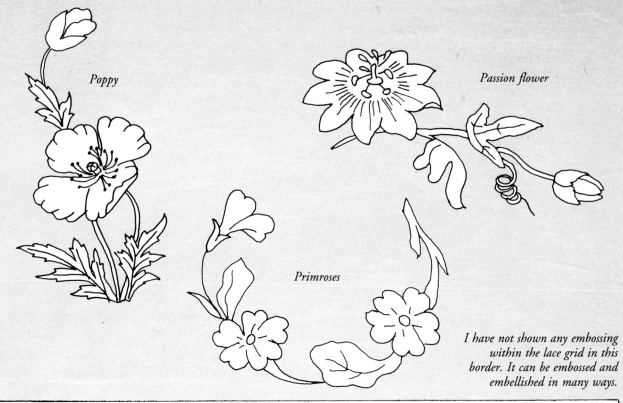

Poppy

Passion flower

Primroses

I have not shown any embossing within the lace grid in this border. It can be embossed and embellished in many ways.

Tiger lily

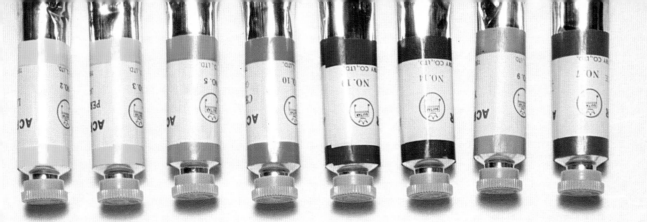

Using acrylic paints

To get the right effect on parchment paper, paints must be transparent, so acrylic paints must be used as dilute washes. Take a little colour from a wet palette and mix washes on a clean white working palette so that you can see the colour you are making; try them out on a spare piece of paper. You may need to add more water (not white) to get a paler shade of colour, or to add just a touch of another colour to get the correct shade. The tiger lily design is used to show the technique.

Materials

Acrylic paints   These usually have a matt finish, but there are several with high gloss effects. I prefer just a hint of shine, but the watercolour technique used does take off the high gloss effect of gloss acrylics.

Wet palette   It is worthwhile investing in a wet palette which will keep your acrylic paints workable for some time; you can even use them the next day depending on how much paint was originally placed on the palette.

Colouring with acrylic paints

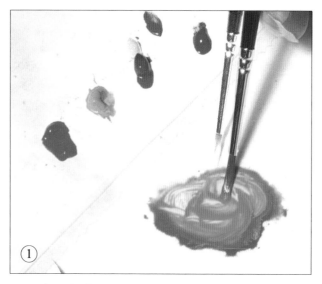

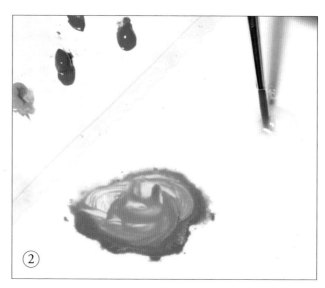

1. Take a little orange paint from the wet palette and mix with water on the working palette to make a thin wash. There is no need to mix colours with white as embossing adds the white to your finished work.

2. If you are using matt paints, place a small amount of gloss medium on to the working palette, pick it up with the brush and then work it into your wash.

3. Pick up the wash with a dryish brush and apply a thin coat to each petal and leaf. This will give you a waterproof base when it is dry. Add successive coats of thinned paint to give transparent shaded effects. Mix colour washes on the working palette. Work using a slight circular motion with the brush.

4. Deepen the shadows on the leaves by adding more colour to the original wash.

(5)

(6)

5. Add details such as stamens and anthers using a thin brush and neat burnt umber. Outline the petals carefully.

6. Paint the leaves and stem green and then add detail to the leaves.

Embossing the design

(1)

(2)

1. Remove the pattern and emboss the central areas of the petals from the front using the 3mm tool.

2. Turn the design over and emboss the back of the flower and leaves using the plastic-headed tool.

Passion flower. *The main petals of this design are only faintly coloured so trace the petals with white ink and then use a wash with the merest hint of colour. Add a little more colour to the wash for the shaded areas, and another dash to paint the bud and the main lines in the flower.*

Poppy. *Use a thin crimson wash for the base of the petals and then add a little more red to the wash to obtain the shading colour. Use a mix of dark and light green together with blue and burnt umber for the leaves.*

Primrose. *Use a yellow wash, and then add the merest touch of red to give a golden hue for the shading and the tiny lines in the petals.*

Tiger lily. *When outlining the petals, do not make the lines too heavy; simply define the petal shapes and then shade in using a slightly darker wash.*

Border design

The basic border design given on page 58 can be customised in many ways; you can cut all or some of the 4-needle grid to crosses and slots; add some embossed dots; include freehand stylus line work and 3-needle, 7-needle and half-circle tool work. When customising patterns, always try out part of the modified design on spare pieces of paper. Keep these scraps with the pattern for future reference.

The marking stage of lace borders is most important because, if you make a mistake, it is impossible to correct it. Although I am not particularly proud of the border on the card below, I have decided to include it to illustrate how a lapse in concentration can affect the end result – note the uneven slots!

The finished tiger lily in its lace border. I have amended the border design by adding embossed dots, freehand stylus work and some 3- and 7-needle work.

Victorian pansies

This card has a Victorian flavour about it. The oval is attached to the lace background with tiny blobs of silicone glue behind the fancy embossed edge, where they will not show through. Victorian cards were single sheets of card with an embellished design on one side and a handwritten message on the other. To create this effect, simply perforate round the whole of the fancy edge of the lace grid and attach it to a stiff piece of coloured card with silicone glue.

Making the oval element

Trace the fancy border with white ink and the single-line oval with gold.

Using a thin wash of ultramarine and crimson, paint in the upper two petals of each pansy. Use a lemon wash for the other petals and then give them an edge with the first colour, using the brush in a circular motion. Darken the first wash with a little ultramarine and use this to draw in the fine lines.

Pattern for oval element. It is reproduced at 80%. Enlarge it by 125% to get a full-size pattern.

Mix some red and yellow for the flower centres. Use a thin wash of ultramarine for the forget-me-nots and add a dot of yellow in their centres. Use combinations of dark and light green and burnt umber to paint the leaves and stems. Paint the bow with a mixture of lemon and vermillion, then add more vermillion to the wash for the shaded areas, but do not paint the 'insides' of the bow. Colour the back of the oval with cobalt blue oil pastel.

Emboss the longer segments of the frill from the back of the paper and the shorter ones from the front. Gently emboss the flowers and the bow, working the inside parts of the latter from the front of the paper. Finally, perforate round the frilled edge.

64

Making the lace background

If you want to produce this design on a folded card, mark the fold line with a white pencil; some of the lace border edge will extend over the fold line.

Trace the outer frilled edge and the central oval in white ink and the double-rule outer border with gold. Mark the lace grid. Emboss the straight lines in the grid using the 1-needle tool and a ruler. Emboss between the double gold lines and the individual segments of the frilled edge.

Re-perforate the lace grid (only taking the needle tool two-thirds of its length through the paper) and then cut out the centre four-hole part of each block. Pierce a hole at all intersections of the straight lines. Perforate round the frilled edge. (If you are making a folded card, perforate out the small section of the frilled edge that overhangs the fold line before folding the card.) Finally, attach the completed oval element to the background with tiny blobs of silicone glue.

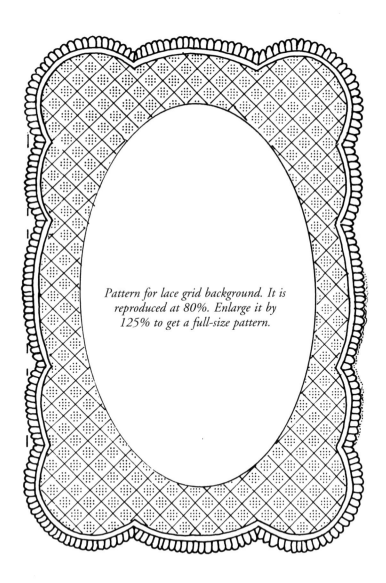

Pattern for lace grid background. It is reproduced at 80%. Enlarge it by 125% to get a full-size pattern.

Here is the finished card. Remember that pansies come in all the colours of the rainbow. Experiment with other colour combinations on the palette – you will be amazed at the number of colours you can create from a limited colour range. The more you practise and experiment, the easier your colour mixing will become.

By using other flowers in the oval segment you get a completely different look to the overall design as you can see from this poppy. I always paint my flowers first and then add the border. This way, if I do not like the colour or the way I have painted it, I will not have wasted too much time and effort. You can put these rejects to good use by experimenting with different border designs.

Three-dimensional objects

Adding a third dimension to parchment work is fun. I use the technique mostly for framed pictures and small boxes but, of course, you can also apply the technique to cards by making extra leaves or petals on spare pieces of paper. Choose foreground shapes that appear to come out of the picture, and play with the arrangement before gluing the pieces in place.

I have chosen one of my favourite flowers, the fuchsia, for the project in this chapter. Fuchsias come in so many different shapes, sizes and colours that I never tire of using them.

The background to the picture is a lace grid arranged round painted stems, leaves and some flower heads. The three-dimensional flowers are painted using the same colours as the flat ones on the background. For each flower you will need one green stamen and six red or purple ones with tiny ends. Buy a bunch of white ones and dip them into ink to colour them – make sure they are dry before you use them.

Making the background

Fix the parchment to the pattern and paint the leaves and stems with acrylic paint or inks. Trace the flowers on the background with very thin red lines. Mark the lace grid. Colour the flowers on the background, on both sides of the paper, with shades of red oil pastel. Use red ink to draw in the stamens and purple ink for the anthers of the shorter stamens. Use watercolour pencils to add shaded areas. Emboss to taste, then re-perforate the lace grid and cut the central grid of each piece to a cross – the rest of each pattern should remain as pricking only.

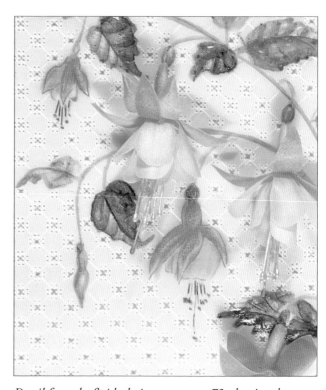

Detail from the finished picture on page 72, showing the painted and embossed background, the lace grid and the three-dimensional flowers.

TIP: Assembling work

Tweezers are invaluable when putting this sort of work together.

TIP: Removing excess glue

To remove any excess silicone glue, wait until it is fully dry and then gently rub with your finger to peel it off.

TIP: After gluing

Check during the first half hour of drying time to ensure that the pieces have remained in place.

Full-size pattern for the base design and border.

Full-size patterns for the pieces of the flower head.

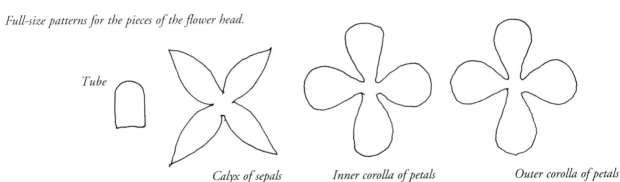

Tube

Calyx of sepals

Inner corolla of petals

Outer corolla of petals

Making the flower heads

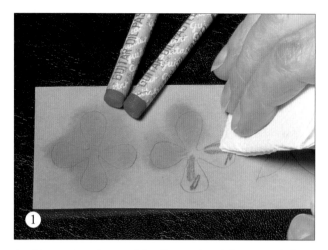

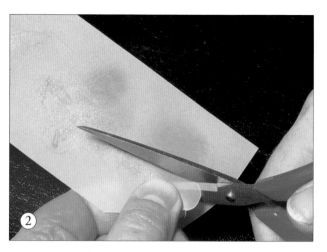

1. Trace the pieces of the flower head (you need three complete heads in all). Colour them, on the back and front of the paper, with shades of red oil pastel. Blend the colour with a piece of kitchen paper.

2. Using a sharp pair of scissors, cut out all the fuchsia pieces.

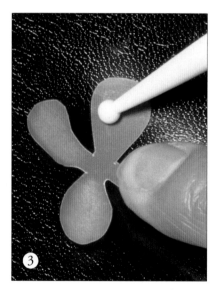

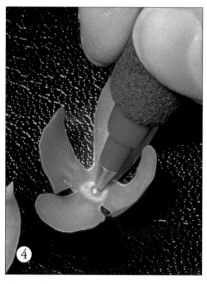

3. Lightly emboss the calyx of sepals and the inner and outer corollas of petals with the 4mm plastic tool until the individual petals start to curl.

4. Emboss the centre of each piece using the 1.5mm tool to make the calyx of sepals and the corollas of petals curl up to the required shape.

5. Make a hole in the centre of each fully embossed piece. Push a stamen through the hole in the inner corolla of petals and, using a cocktail stick, apply glue to the petal and stamen as shown.

6. Slide the outer corolla of petals on to the stamen and, using the blob of glue as a spacer, position it slightly above the inner corolla.

7. Using more small blobs of glue, assemble the calix of sepals. Roll up the tube and glue this so that it is touching the top of the sepals.

8. Add another small blob of glue inside the petals and assemble the rest of the stamens.

9. Glue the completed flower head on to the base design.

The finished three-dimensional fuchsia picture. If your flower heads do not lie exactly as you want them to, carefully cut off the two sepals at the back, glue the trimmed flower head on to the background and then attach the two sepals in the required positions.

72

Orchid box

Making a box is another wonderful way of using your parchment craft skills. If you can bear to part with it, the recipient will be overjoyed and you can be sure that the box will be kept long after any contents have been discarded.

If you want to design your own box, carefully take apart a favourite container and use this as the basis for a pattern. Always try out new patterns with plain parchment paper; you may have to make minor alterations. When you are happy with the outline pattern, decorate it to your own taste. Remember that the same basic shape can be used many times and can be decorated in different ways.

To get you started I have included the pattern of the hexagonal box below which is decorated with a lace grid and three-dimensional orchids.

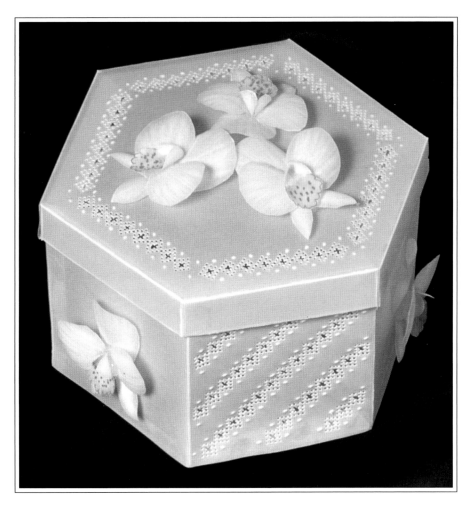

Try your hand at making this box, with its simple orchid and lace work decorations. I am indebted to Doug Little for designing the ingenious box shell that fits together easily and to Marilyn Owen for designing the 'beginners' orchids which I have used to decorate the box.

Making the box and lid

Using a white pencil, draw the outlines and the folds of the box and lid on to a sheet of paper.

On the back of the paper, colour the lid and the plain sides of the box with green-grey oil pastel. Colour the other sides of the box with light orange oil pastel.

Place the paper back on the pattern and mark the lace grids. Emboss the design in the lace grid. Re-perforate and cut the central area of each small block to a cross.

Place double-sided sticky tape on the base flaps (F) and side tab (T). Cut out the box and lid, emboss the fold lines with a stylus and crease along the fold lines.

Stick the sides together with tab (T) and then stick the base flaps (F) to the inside of each side. Fold in the flaps at the top of the sides.

Fold the sides of the lid down and slot in the tabs; there is no need to use sticky tape as the ingenious folding holds it together.

The patterns on this page are reproduced at 80%. Enlarge by 125% to get full-size patterns.

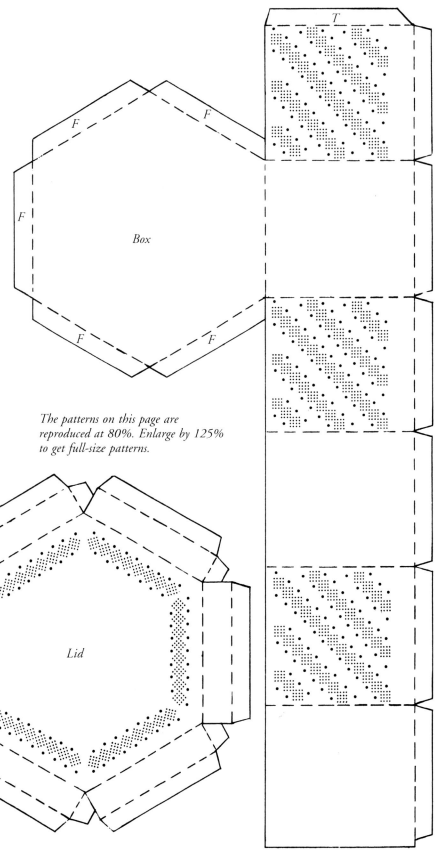

74

Making the orchids

Trace the three pieces needed for each orchid with white pencil (you need six complete orchids for the whole box). Paint the orchid throats (shape 3) first with orange and then with red ink – both watered down. Use a spotter brush with undiluted ink to put on the dots.

Perforate round the crimped edge of the throat and cut through the perforations so that your orchid ends up with a realistic throat. Cut round the outline of shapes 1 and 2.

Emboss the top half of the large petal (shape 1) from the back of the paper, using first the 4mm plastic tool and then the 3mm steel tool. Use the stylus tool to finish off, working from the middle to the top of each petal in straight lines and keeping each line close to the previous one to give a veined effect.

Emboss the double petals (shape 2) from the back of the paper and again finish off with the stylus to give a veined effect near the trumpet area.

Emboss the crimped edge of the throat from the front of the paper, working from the middle to the outer edge.

Turn down the two tiny flaps on the throat so that they come over the painted throat. Use a cocktail stick to place a blob of silicone glue just above the two tiny petals on shape 1, and in the middle of shape 2. Carefully assemble the flowers. Leave to dry for at least two hours, preferably over night.

Use silicone glue to mount three orchids on the box lid and one on each of the plain sides of the box. Leave your work to dry for at least two hours.

Full-size pattern for three-dimensional orchids.

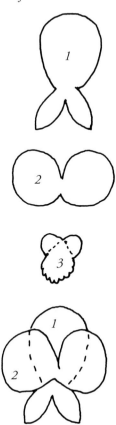

Detail of three-dimensional orchids.

Christmas tree

This tree is a real show-stopper for your Christmas mantelpiece or windowsill. It takes time to make, so do not leave it until the last minute. It consists of six circular designs which, after being coloured, embossed and perforated, are folded into conical shapes and mounted on a central cone. I found a small star to embellish the top of the tree.

Making the central cone

Trace the cone outline in white pencil, then colour in the cone with oil pastel. Put some narrow double-sided tape on to the tab and then cut round the complete shape. Gently roll the cone until it easily takes up a curved shape. Remove the protective paper from the sticky tape and complete the cone shape.

Preparing the layers of the tree

Following the patterns on pages 78–9, use a white pencil to mark out the lines and the circles for each layer of the tree. Mark the lace grids.

Colour the central area of each layer with deep green oil pastel. Work from the back of the paper only. Leave the borders uncoloured.

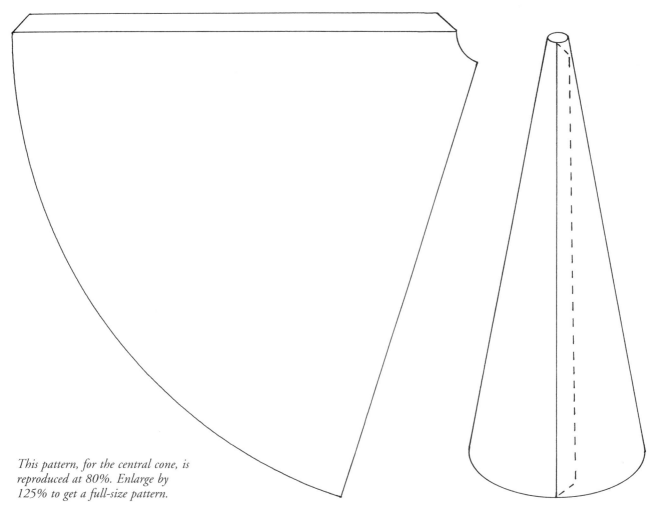

This pattern, for the central cone, is reproduced at 80%. Enlarge by 125% to get a full-size pattern.

Emboss the patterns in the lace grids. Free-hand emboss the tiny dots that complete the top of the white border.

Re-perforate and cut to crosses the lace grids in the centre of the borders and those at the top of the triangular border edge. Cut through the outside perforations to make the edge of the border. Perforate out the central circle and remove the waste paper.

Assembling the tree

Each layer is marked with concertina fold lines radiating out from the centre; the broken lines are the valleys and the solid ones the peaks. Emboss the broken lines on the front of the paper and the solid lines on the back. Carefully crease along each line, easing the layer into a shallow conical shape.

To make the tree look as if it has a little frost on it, put tiny dabs of clear nail varnish on to the layers and sprinkle with ultrafine crystal glitter. If you work over a piece of scrap paper, you can put any spare glitter back into the bottle when you have finished.

Slide the completed layers of the tree on to the cone and ease them into place.

Apply a blob of silicone glue round the top inner edge of the cone and position the star. Leave to dry.

The patterns on these pages are reproduced at 80%. Enlarge by 125% to get full-size patterns.

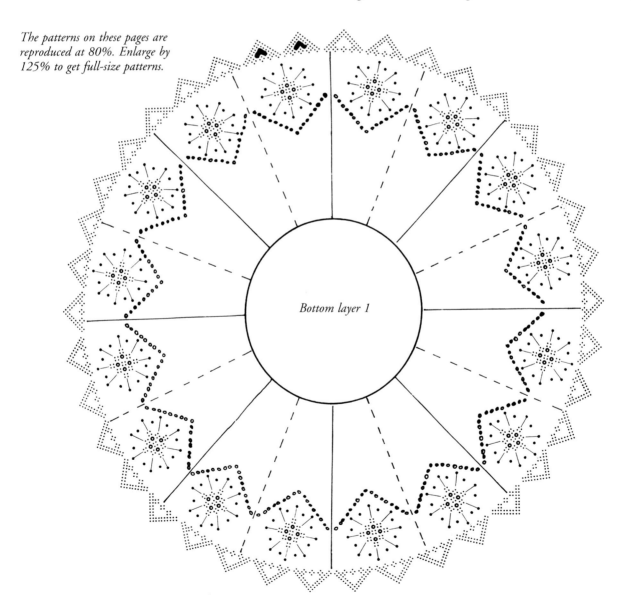

Bottom layer 1

Top
layer 6

Intermediate
layer 3

Intermediate
layer 4

Intermediate
layer 5

Intermediate layer 2

Conclusion

I do hope that you have enjoyed this book. Although it is the basic techniques of tracing, embossing and lace work that are the most important elements of this ancient and beautiful craft, colouring is also a feature. Do experiment with materials as there are no hard and fast rules as to what can and cannot be used to colour your work. In some South American countries where this craft has been practised for over four hundred years (long before acrylic paints and inks or any other such modern colouring mediums were even thought of), oil pastels, watercolour pencils and pencil crayons are used. Other South American countries produce the most wonderful lace-like cards using no colour at all. Techniques and styles differ so much from one South American country to the next, that it would need another book to cover them all.

Index